This
Read, Listen, & Wonder
book belongs to:

_____

_____

_____

CANDLEWICK PRESS

For my grandfather, S.H.K., with love
V. F.
For Robert and Chloe
C. V.

Text copyright © 1993 by Vivian French
Illustrations copyright © 1993 by Charlotte Voake

First U.S. paperback edition with CD 2010

The Library of Congress has cataloged the hardcover edition as follows:

French, Vivian
Caterpillar, caterpillar / by Vivian French ;
illustrated by Charlotte Voake. —1st U.S. ed.
Summary: A girl learns about caterpillars and butterflies as she watches
her grandfather grow them on the nettles in his garden.
ISBN 978-1-56402-206-6 (hardcover)
1. Caterpillars—juvenile literature. 2. Butterflies—Development—Juvenile literature. [1. Butterflies. 2. Caterpillars.
3. Metamorphusis.]
I. Voake, Charlotte, ill. II. Title. III. Series: Read and wonder.
QL544.2.F74 1993
595.78'904334—dc20 92-54406

ISBN 978-1-56402-493-0 (paperback)
ISBN 978-0-7636-4002-6 (paperback with CD)

09 10 11 12 13 14 SWT 10 9 8 7 6 5 4 3 2 1

Printed in Dongguan, Guangdong, China

This book was typeset in Calligraphic 810 BT.
The illustrations were done in pen and watercolor.

Candlewick Press
99 Dover Street
Somerville, Massachusetts 02144

visit us at www.candlewick.com

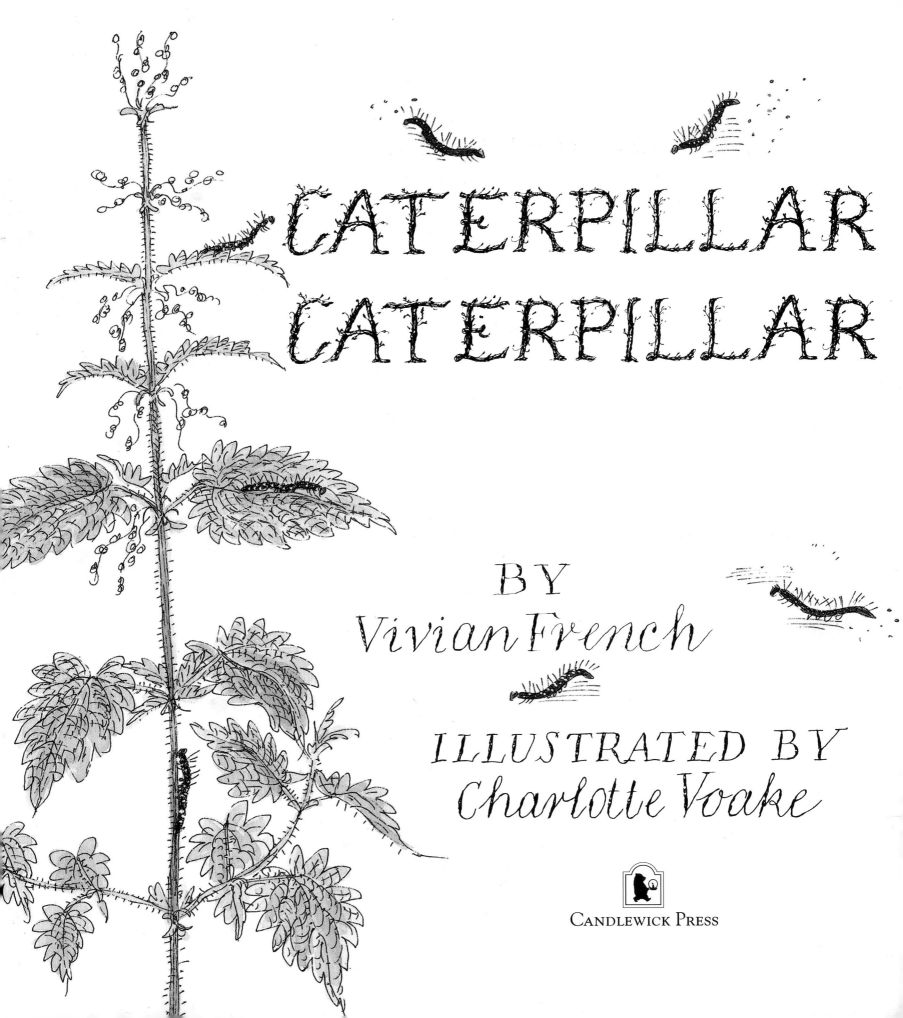

CATERPILLAR
CATERPILLAR

BY

Vivian French

ILLUSTRATED BY

Charlotte Voake

CANDLEWICK PRESS

My father and my grandfather both liked gardening very much, but my grandfather used to grow stinging nettles. My father didn't; he said they were weeds, and rooted them out.

"Why don't you get rid of your nettles?" I asked my grandfather.

"Stinging nettles grow butterflies," he said. "Go and look."

I went and looked. I couldn't see any butterflies, though. My grandfather turned one of the nettle leaves over to show me the bumps on the back of it, but I didn't know what they were.

"Butterfly eggs," said my grandfather.

"What kind of butterflies?"

My grandfather peered closely at the bumps.

"I don't have my glasses on," he said, "but they could

be tortoiseshells, or peacocks. They both like nettles.

If you keep an eye on them you'll see when

the caterpillars hatch."

"Won't they crawl away?" I asked.

My grandfather straightened up

and looked down at me.

"Humph," he said.

"You just keep watching."

So I did.

NETTLES WILL STING YOU IF YOU TOUCH THEM, BUT THEY WON'T STING THE CATERPILLARS.

THE EGGS ARE DOME-SHAPED, WITH LITTLE RIDGES. EACH EGG IS ABOUT THE SIZE OF THE TOP OF A PIN.

MOST BUTTERFLIES LAY THEIR EGGS IN ONES AND TWOS, MOVING FROM PLANT TO PLANT. PEACOCK AND TORTOISESHELL BUTTERFLIES LAY LOTS OF EGGS AT ONCE.

Nothing happened at all for two days. It rained very hard on the second day, but the eggs were still safe.

The next day there were lots and lots
of little tiny caterpillars crawling on the
nettle leaves: The eggs were papery
and empty. I squashed some
with my fingernail.

THE CATERPILLARS EAT
THEIR WAY OUT OF THE
EGGS WHEN THEY'RE
READY TO HATCH,
AND STAY TOGETHER
IN A BIG CROWD.

THEY MAKE A WEB OF
WHITE SILK BETWEEN
THE STEM OF THE PLANT
AND THE LEAVES.
IT'S LIKE A TENT.

WHEN THEY'VE EATEN
ALL THE LEAVES NEARBY,
THEY MOVE ON AND
MAKE A NEW TENT.

My grandfather came over to see

what I was doing.

"Ah," he said, "peacock caterpillars."

"Do they eat cabbage?" I asked.

I'd seen caterpillars on cabbages.

He shook his head. "Caterpillars are fussy eaters. If you put a nettle-eating caterpillar on a cabbage, it'll set off to look for nettles, and if it can't find any, it'll sit down and die rather than eat cabbage."

SOME OF THE CATERPILLARS YOU SEE ON CABBAGES ARE

ORANGE TIP CATERPILLARS EAT LADY'S-SMOCK AND GARLIC MUSTARD. (SOMETIMES THEY EAT EACH OTHER.)

COMMA CATERPILLARS LIKE HOPS BEST, BUT SOMETIMES THEY HAVE TO MAKE DO WITH NETTLES.

CABBAGE WHITES. THEY LOVE CABBAGE.

PEACOCK, SMALL TORTOISESHELL, AND RED ADMIRAL CATERPILLARS ALL LIKE NETTLES BEST.

THE CATERPILLARS LEAVE LITTLE DROPPINGS WHEREVER THEY GO.

AS THEY GET BIGGER, YOU CAN SEE THEIR WHITE SPOTS MORE CLEARLY.

THEY DON'T MIND WHICH WAY UP THEY EAT, AND THEY HARDLY EVER STOP EATING.

I looked at my peacock caterpillars.
They were all together in a little
crowd, eating as fast as they could.

"Won't the birds eat them?" I asked.

"Couldn't we cover them up?"

"No need," said my grandfather.

"Caterpillars that don't hide away are really saying,
'I'm poisonous—keep off!' And the birds know that."

He pulled his pipe out of his pocket and very,
very gently nudged one of the caterpillars.
It curled itself up at once and fell off the leaf.

"There," he said. "Even if something does come along
looking for a snack, the caterpillar might still escape."

"Can I make one curl up?" I stuck my finger out.

"Don't touch them," my grandfather said.

"Some spiny caterpillars can give you a rash,
and other kinds leave a bad smell on
your fingers. Besides, you might hurt them."

THEY HAVE VELVETY BODIES AND SHINY HEADS.
LOOK AT THEIR SPINY BACKS!
THEY HAVE THREE PAIRS OF LEGS
IN FRONT, WITH LITTLE
CLAWS ON THEM, AND
STUMPIER LEGS DOWN.
EARTHER DOWN.

I went on watching the caterpillars.

They were getting bigger. By the second Saturday in July they had eaten almost all the plant they had hatched on and were crawling over the other nettles.

Some of them were lying completely still, though, and not eating at all. All of a sudden one of them gave a little wriggle, and its skin split right open. Inside was another brand-new caterpillar, and it crawled out of the old skin as if it were crawling out of a sleeping bag. It looked very fresh and clean, and it seemed to be bigger than before. All the other caterpillars changed skins too.

WHEN THEY'RE READY TO CHANGE THEIR SKIN, CATERPILLARS SPIN A LITTLE SILK MAT ON THE LEAF AND FASTEN THEIR LAST TWO LEGS TO IT.

I knew something must be eating my caterpillars, because by now there weren't so many of them.

I didn't mind that, but I did mind five days later when I found that every single one of them had disappeared.

"Where have they gone?" I asked. I was close to tears. "Pea sticks," said my grandfather. We marched around the corner of the shed to where the pea sticks were.

"Sometimes one or two come here," my grandfather said.

"Ah, yes, here we are." Sure enough, there was one of the caterpillars, hanging head downward off a pea stick. And to my amazement, before my very eyes, its skin began to peel off from its head upward . . . and shrivel away.

This time there wasn't another caterpillar ready to come out. Instead there was something like a little soft brown bag, hanging on the pea stick. It didn't have legs or eyes or anything, and it dried up into a little case.

My grandfather said that was just what it was,

but the proper name for it was a pupa or chrysalis.

"But where's the caterpillar gone?" I asked.

All the bits of caterpillar were inside the case,

he said, and they were changing.

WHEN THEY'RE READY TO PUPATE, THE CATERPILLARS LEAVE THEIR NETTLES.

EACH ONE OF THEM FINDS A PLACE TO BE ON THEIR OWN.

IT MIGHT BE UP A TREE, A FENCE, A STICK, OR A TWIG.

THEY MAKE
A TINY WHITE
PAD...

THEN THEY
ATTACH THEIR
BACK LEGS TO
IT AND HANG
UPSIDE DOWN.

SOON THEIR SKIN PEELS
OFF, LEAVING BEHIND
A BEAUTIFUL PUPA.
IT'S GREEN IF IT'S ON
A LEAF AND BROWN
IF IT'S ON A
TWIG.

Just this once, I was allowed to bring the stick with the little case on it into the kitchen. I watched for ten whole days, and on the tenth day the pupa got very, very dark.

The next morning I was eating my breakfast when my grandfather suddenly said, "LOOK!"

I rushed to see, and the case of the pupa

had split. Something was crawling out . . .

but it didn't look at all like a butterfly.

It was crumpled, and it looked damp,

and it wasn't at all a pretty color.

"It must have gone wrong,"

I said, feeling very sad.

Very gently, my grandfather
lifted the stick and put it on
the windowsill in the sunshine.
The creature crawled slowly up
the stick and stopped.
Little by little it began to stretch out.
It was just like watching a flower
unfolding itself, only it had
wings instead of petals.

THE WINGS
OF THE
BUTTERFLY
UNFOLD AS LIQUID
IS PUMPED INTO
ITS VEINS.
THEY HAVE TO
DRY FOR AN
HOUR OR TWO
BEFORE IT
CAN FLY.

And the wings began to tremble, and to shine in the sunlight, and then suddenly there it was—a real butterfly, with spidery legs, and its wings spread wide open.

It was so lovely that I couldn't say anything at all. Then its wings fluttered and it flew off into the garden—the very newest butterfly there.

VIVIAN FRENCH has written dozens of books for children, including *The Robe of Skulls* and *Growing Frogs*. As a child, she watched with her grandfather as a family of tiny caterpillar eggs turned, stage by stage, into beautiful butterflies. Vivian French lives in Edinburgh, Scotland.

CHARLOTTE VOAKE has written and illustrated many books for young children, including *Ginger, Pizza Kittens,* and *Hello Twins,* which was a *New York Times Book Review* Best Illustrated Children's Book of the Year. Charlotte Voake lives in Surrey, England.